Rebel Writer's Workbook

A practical guide to focus your intentions, set result-oriented goals, and manifest the creative life of your dreams.

Libby Copa

Disclaimer

All information in this book is based on the wit, whims, and education of the author, Libby Copa. The information is intended to motivate you Rebels; however, you should make your own decisions and do follow-up research before making any major life decisions, obviously.

Copyright

Cover Art and Author Image by Tarn Ellis

ISBN 978-1-7351183-0-7

For more cool writing-related stuff, visit: www.LibbyCopa.com

"'Hey Johnny, what are you rebelling against?' 'Whaddya got?'" -The Wild Ones, 1953

Welcome, Rebel. I'm glad you're here.

I've always been somewhat of a rebel: I was born early, I went to alternative schools for almost all of my schooling, I told my government job to suck it, and I began living an artist life and have been doing that for years now. I haven't ever wanted to be like everyone else–tradition always felt really boring to me.

"So now you're here, telling me what to do?" No, not really. This is more of a spirit guide thing than a life manual. You'll make it what you need it to be.

"Who are you to lead me?" I don't know, man. All I can say is I've been where you are and I found a way out, or in, or around it, or whatever. You can take this map as far as you want it. You will undoubtedly make it your own crazy journey. You will go off this map and go your own way. I'm just here to help get you going. I'm a Rebel–I love to push a little bit, or a lot, even if that means having to push another Rebel.

"But seriously, why you?" Like I said, I've been that writer searching for a way to create a writer's life, to thrive as an artist. I published my first poem in an acclaimed literary journal at eighteen and I thought, "That's it, I've made it." Ha! If only it were that easy. I didn't publish again for years. But I'm a persistent Rebel and kept with it, kept educating myself, kept putting myself out there, and now have dozens of published pieces out in the world. For over a decade I've been helping others strengthen their own writing as an editor and writing coach. I've been teaching creative writing to Rebels and non-Rebels alike in all the communities I've ever thrived in. I'm living my life as a writer and creator.

Are you ready to join me?
Are you ready to live your life as a Rebel and a Writer? A Rebel Writer?

How this workbook works:

There's ample evidence out there that tells us that writing in a journal creates clarity of mind and refines goals. It helps to release negative energy and build up motivation. Just go to YouTube and search "journal." You'll see the many topics that come up. It works. That being said, I've never been a fan of journaling. As I write I always think, would my time be better spent writing a poem? Am I just doing this so I don't have to focus on writing another chapter of my dystopian young adult novel? It was never for me, and I couldn't keep with it for long. But what I found that I *did* like were *guided* journals. Being asked a question. Being given a goal. Straight up telling me to write down what I wanted to manifest into being.

That's my aspiration here—to have you focus your intentions toward your writing goals and your artist dream life. To give you insight into the publishing world and help you decide how you may want to be a part of it.

I want to be encouraging, but I want to be realistic. That's why this is a workbook—not a journal. It can be done in chunks or one question a day. If you aren't feeling a topic, skip it and come back to it later. No biggie. It's up to you how quickly you want to move through this book and build the momentum to change your life.

Remember this is from my education, my experience, and the experiences I've witnessed in hundreds of other writers over the years. But it might not all ring true for you. Take what resonates with you and dumpster-fire-burn the rest.

This workbook is a practical guide to help you make your dreams a reality. I don't want to bore you with a bunch of stories or take up your time hiding the details in long-windedness. I want you to have quick wins. I want to motivate you, not wear you out so you won't have the energy to go work on your writing project afterward.

Let's get your focus clear and get you manifesting your dream life.
Let's get you writing.

"I write to discover. I write to uncover. I write to meet my ghosts . . ."
-Terry Tempest Williams

We all have our own journeys: what led us to where we are now, what shaped us to have the goals we've set forth for ourselves. These are stories we hold. These struggles and excitements are what we intentionally or unintentionally write about. We weren't always writers, but we are now.

When did you start writing? How did you get here? Did you always want to be a writer?

Why is writing important to you?

What is your favorite part about writing?

What aspects of writing do you find easiest?

What aspects of writing do you find hardest?

When you're stalled with what to write about, what are three steps you'll take right away to overcome your writer's block?

Stephen King said, "If you don't have time to read, you don't have the time (or the tools) to write. Simple as that." You've probably seen this quoted a thousand times on Twitter. The reason it's quoted so frequently is because it's the truth. Reading is the ultimate education to help you become a better writer. Read as often as you can and as much as you can. Consume books at the rate you consume food or air. It's my No. 1 piece of advice for getting where you want to go as a writer. But don't just read in your favorite genres or the genre in which you write—read the rainbow. Read from around the world. Read traditional and indie. Read bestsellers and not.

Which book has had the biggest impact on your life?

I am committed to reading _____ books a year.

The next three books I'm committed to reading are:

What's your favorite part about reading? Does your writing reflect that love?

"Rebels and nonconformists are often the pioneers and designers of change."
-Indira Gandhi

Writing with intention is what can lead a book to change the world. But your mission doesn't always have to be to change the world, or even to change a person deeply. Your desire may be to make the reader laugh, cry, or heal. You always have to know what your intention is when sharing a story.

Do current politics influence your writing? Does your spirituality? Do you have a political, moral, spiritual, or social agenda when you write?

Do you write anything that might be viewed as controversial?

Do you want readers to feel something specific, think something specific, or change something after reading your work?

Do you want to educate, inspire, or both?

What is your deepest hope the outcome will be after a reader finishes reading your writing?

What makes your writing unique? How will your writing stand out? What are you offering readers that they haven't found elsewhere?

Who has influenced your writing the most over the years?

What's the most surprising thing you've learned from your own writing?

Fear can often hold us hostage from being able to create. It can prevent us from sharing our writing because of what we imagine might happen to us if we share our story, even a story we've made up. We might worry about being judged or abandoned because of our creative pursuits. We can let what-ifs keep us from our dreams.

What do you imagine is the worst outcome after you put your writing into the world?

What do your family and friends think of your writing goals? Who stands in your way by being unsupportive? Who is in your corner?

What stories do you know your family or friends would not want you to tell?

What stories would you be embarrassed for your family or friends to read?

How will you address or ignore those unsupportive of your craft?

"Vision without action is merely a dream. Action without vision just passes the time. Vision with action can change the world."
-Joel A. Barker

Writing is hard. It takes a lot of time and care. It's not for the weak of heart. You must be able to accept rejection, and you must seek out rejection. The literary world is a *world* of rejection, but seeing your work in print—there's really nothing like it.

What I've observed with those around me is the more you put into it—writing time, building community, going to writing events, reading—the more you'll get out of it. The writers I've witnessed build careers with their art didn't make it happen overnight. They worked for it. They were in writing groups. They got their writing rejected, a lot. They shared what they knew with other writers in some way—teaching, critique groups, interacting/supporting other writers, going to writers conferences, and asking questions.

For me to build a career as an editor took a long, long time. I was doing it well before I was paid to do it, and then when I started getting paid to do it, I was still working other jobs as well. It took time to build up my client list, to earn referrals from those clients, to be able to leave a full-time position for my artist life, as I dreamily call it.

What has worked for me to make forward motion with my writing and career as an editor is setting yearly goals for myself. These are realistic goals that if I put the time and care into, I can achieve them with ease (being able to achieve them is a big motivator). I don't start with a list of unattainable goals: write three books this year, get an agent, get a publisher, get in *The New Yorker*. I start smaller with one goal, and I break it down into even smaller goals. You want to achieve a writing career in the next decade? Break down what you think it'll take to get there and then break those goals down, then break those goals down even more until you see a clear path ahead of you for this one year, this one month, this one week.

It might look something like this:

Big goal: Win an award for my short story collection

Goal before that: Publish a short story collection
Goal before that: Sell a short story collection
Goal before that: Find an agent
Goal before that: Win a Pushcart Prize for a short story
Goal before that: Publish a short story in a literary journal
Goal before that: Submit to literary journals
Goal before that: Revise a short story
Goal before that: Have a short story edited
Goal before that: Receive critique group feedback on a story
Goal before that: Find a critique group
Goal before that: Write a short story
Goal before that: Sit down and write

See what I mean?

Play with breaking down a big goal you have.

My big goal: _____

_____

Break it down:

What are other supporting goals you have for your writing life?

Do you want to make a career out of writing? Do you want writing to be a hobby? Do you want writing to be a part of your life or your whole life? Do you have lots of stories you want to tell, or just one story?

What author has the writing life you dream of having? What aspects do you love about how they've established themselves as a writer?

On average, how much time do you spend on your creative life each day?

⌇⌇⌇⌇⌇⌇⌇⌇⌇⌇⌇⌇⌇⌇⌇⌇⌇⌇⌇⌇⌇⌇⌇⌇⌇⌇⌇⌇⌇⌇⌇⌇⌇⌇⌇⌇⌇

Ideally, how much time do you wish to spend pursuing your creative life each day?

⌇⌇⌇⌇⌇⌇⌇⌇⌇⌇⌇⌇⌇⌇⌇⌇⌇⌇⌇⌇⌇⌇⌇⌇⌇⌇⌇⌇⌇⌇⌇⌇⌇⌇⌇⌇⌇

How would your dream day be balanced?

12:00 AM	
1:00 AM	
2:00 AM	
3:00 AM	
4:00 AM	
5:00 AM	
6:00 AM	
7:00 AM	
8:00 AM	
9:00 AM	
10:00 AM	
11:00 AM	
12:00 PM	
1:00 PM	
2:00 PM	
3:00 PM	
4:00 PM	
5:00 PM	
6:00 PM	
7:00 PM	
8:00 PM	
9:00 PM	
10:00 PM	
11:00 PM	

I'm not going to tell you that you need to create a special space to write that next bestselling, award-winning novel—you can write anywhere: on the bus, in your basement, dictating it to yourself as you drive and transcribing it later. But, I am going to ask you to identify where you've been in the past when you were very successful with getting words down on the page.

What are three locations where you've had good writing sessions? Where were you when inspiration hit?

What do you need to change in your life to allow you to get closer to your goals?

What are three things you can do tomorrow to help you get closer to reaching your writing goals?

Do you have to live in New York City to write or work in the publishing industry? No! You can write anywhere, and there are now publishing houses all over the world with more and more employers transitioning to an online workspace.

Do you need an MFA in creative writing to write or work in publishing? No! I have an MFA in creative writing and the biggest thing I learned from that experience is that you don't need one to be a writer or work in the industry. I'm not knocking my writing degree; there's valuable education and connection-building in these programs. I'm just saying having an MFA is not the be-all and end-all. Remember that quote from *Good Will Hunting*? "You dropped $150,000 on a f****** education you coulda got for $1.50 in late fees at the public library." It's kinda like that.

Do you need to sell out to get a traditional contract? No! Sometimes the publishing world makes you think you need to do this or that, but you don't.

Should you become a teacher so you have more time to write? No! Teachers have heavy workloads. It doesn't guarantee time or energy to write. Be a teacher because you want to help others. If you want to write, be a writer.

If you're interested in working in the publishing industry as, say, a literary agent, editor at a publishing house, or as a publicity manager, then you need to get yourself an internship. The earlier the better. They require far too many hours for someone working or in school and usually pay nothing, but if you start interning in a publishing house, that's your way in the door. Get in the door young if you can. Give them your blood and sweat, and that experience will reward you. But there's never only one way into a building (or into a career).

Creative writing is a muscle that you need to work at in order to strengthen. You never stop searching for what can make you a better writer. You find this knowledge in books, classes, professionals, and peers.

Who do you already know that's working in the publishing world? List the professionals and creatives that you already know. What connections to the writing world do you already have?

What skills and knowledge do you need to gain to reach your writing-related goals?

Where can you grow your skills? What classes can you take to gain more knowledge? Who can you talk to that may be able to give you information you need to strengthen your writing muscles and help you reach your goals?

What inspires you?

What five-minute action can you do right now to get closer to achieving your goals? Maybe send a letter to an author friend asking how she found her agent, or create an email list of people you want to reach out to who may be able to help you reach your writing goals. Sign up for a class. Send a poem to a friend for peer critique. What can you do to give yourself a quick win today?

For many years, indie publishing has gotten a lot of shit—largely from the traditional publishing world. But self-publishing used to be the ultimate Rebel act. It's how people rose up against their monarchs and spread information that the governments didn't want out there. It's *still* a Rebel act, but not as controversial.

"You can't make money." "You can't live off your writing." "The books aren't good enough," *they* say. But all those things can also be said in the traditional publishing world as well. And just because *they* say it, does that make it true?

Andy Weir, Hugh Howey, Christopher Paolini, H.M. Ward, and E.L. freaking James started as indie authors. Crossover from indie to traditional is incredibly rare, but it isn't impossible. That said, if you choose to be an indie author, you should be settled in your heart that you may *always* be an indie author. If that doesn't sit well with you, you shouldn't be self-publishing until you're proud to be in that world.

Indie publishing is about the hustle, and we Rebels already know a thing or two about that. You have to be able to sell yourself. You have to be proud of your book and ready to talk about it, ready to tweet about it in thousands of creative, different ways. You have to seek out your support team. You have to spend some of your own money up front. But then you get to keep all the money after. Yay!

Traditional publishing is still where a lot of the big money sits. For now. It's still the place where the film rights get sold before the book is on the shelves. It's still where Oprah's book club books come from. But it's not the only home anymore. It's not the only audience.

For many Rebels, the appeal of indie publishing is that they continue to have complete control of their book throughout the entire publishing process. Working with a publisher can lead to your book being represented in a way you don't approve of, with a cover you didn't pick, with revisions you didn't love making. Yet the appeal of a traditional publisher's bookstore distribution, their carrying of the costs, and having a professional company in your court, can be enticing to many. Each writer must decide for themselves their own needs and desires, based on what's important to them.

How do you define success?

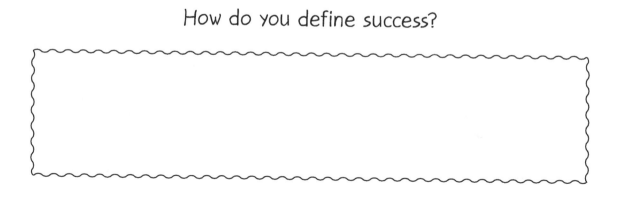

What did success look like when you were younger? What does success look like to you now?

Who are your favorite authors? Who represents those authors? Who publishes their books?

Author	Agent	Publisher

What do you look forward to happening when your book is
published?

What are you afraid of happening when your book is published?

What publishing path do you plan to take?

Regardless of whether you indie publish or traditionally publish, you'll have to present yourself as an author to the world. These days, social media is the most prevalent place for self-promotion.

Will you use a pen name? List your ideas here.

Practice your signature. How will you sign your books for readers?

How do you brand yourself as an author? What is your motto or catch phrase? Do you have a logo?

Which author's social media accounts do you admire? Why are you drawn to their pages? Will you try to mirror their style on your own social media accounts?

Do you already represent yourself as a writer on your social media accounts? What actions can you take now to establish a more professional writer vibe on social media?

"If you want to change the world, find someone to help you paddle."
-William H. McRaven

Expanding your community is essential to developing, strengthening, and selling your book. Your community can be readers of your manuscript, but can also be writing-related conferences, readings, workshops, or groups you attend.

My three biggest supports are:

Find three new beta readers to help strengthen your manuscript. My three new beta readers are:

Find three new critique partners to help strengthen your writing. My three new critique partners are:

Three writing events in my community I am committed to attending in the next three months (poetry slams, book readings, writing conferences, book festivals, open mic nights, etc.):

I encourage you to speak to one stranger about *anything* at each event you attend. Try to make a connection. It doesn't always spark, but you never know—you might just meet your new favorite critique partner or the sister of your future agent.

Do any fears arise when you imagine attending these events in your community?

"An essential aspect of creativity is not being afraid to fail."
- Edwin Land

Accepting that your manuscript is not and will never be perfect is part of the writing game. There's always something you can find to change and that others will suggest you change. Sometimes the feedback is good. Sometimes it's not so good. Learning to thoughtfully listen and apply feedback is an art in itself, and learning to let go of the negative feelings that come along with hearing criticism takes practice.

Honestly, how do you handle constructive criticism?

The mantras below are meant to help you release anger and sadness that might come up when you get a manuscript back with a bunch of red marks on it or get a negative book review.

Practice these mantras by writing them down two times to help you memorize them so they'll be with you when you need them.

I can hear criticism, release it, and move on.		

I get to decide what's right for my manuscript.		
I'll never be able to please everyone, and that's okay.		
Writing is a form of art, and all art is never understood by everyone.		
My manuscript deserves thoughtful alterations.		
My manuscript is growing into its best form.		
I write for myself first.		
Not everyone will be my reader.		

"I believe in putting a rocket of desire out into the universe. And you get it when you believe it."
-Jim Carrey

Visualization is a powerful tool. Olympians use it before their races to imagine themselves crossing the finish line. Actors use it to manifest the income they wish to earn for their next film. Authors use it to clear the path to them holding a hardcover copy of their book in their hands.

When you write out these exercises, I want you to feel yourself in the future moment. Feel it in your body what it would be like to be there. Focus on the vibrations caused by your words.

Visualize yourself giving a speech at a graduation ceremony, TEDx conference, or as a keynote speaker for the Association of Writers & Writing Programs. What would you speak about? What wisdom would you share with others? Write the speech out as if you had to give the speech tomorrow.

Sit down and have an interview with your future self as if you were at a book festival, on a podcast, on National Public Radio, or being interviewed by Oprah. If it feels weird to write both sides of a conversation, it can help to write out all the questions beforehand, but you don't have to. You can go with the flow of the conversation if you want. Read interviews with other authors to get ideas for the conversation.

Questions your interviewer might ask you:

•What are your routines and rituals before you write?
•Do you know the ending before you start writing?
•What are your current writing influences?
•What does your family think of your book?
•How long does it take you to write a book?
•If you weren't a writer, what profession would you like to have?

The Interview:

Visualize yourself at a book festival or con. How would you respond to these different scenarios?

An attendee at the event stops by your booth and asks, "What's your book about?" What is your one-minute pitch?

A young writer approaches you and says, "I want to be a writer someday." How do you respond? What advice do you give them?

A reader walks over to your booth and says, "I tried to read your book, but I only got through a few chapters. I didn't like it." How do you respond?

What will draw readers over to your booth? Will you do a giveaway? Have a mailing list sign-up? A contest? Spin the wheel, win a prize? How will you get them to stop at your booth?

Visualize receiving a letter from a fan. What do they love best about your books? How will they connect with the story you've written?

Dear   ,

Sincerely,

Your biggest fan

Giving back is essential to the human spirit. How will you support other artists when you've achieved your own dream?

Who do you want to connect with now that you're living your dream? With which artists, authors, influencers, actors, or entrepreneurs do you collaborate?

"Young adult books can't have sex or swear words." "A standard self-help book is fifty to sixty thousand words." "There must already be a market for it to sell to a publishing house." "You must write in the same genre for the rest of your career." *They* say a lot of things that aren't rules—maybe guidelines, but not set in stone. Even if there were official rules somewhere, rules are meant to be broken, aren't they, Rebel? Write what you want to write, how you want to write it.

What do you want to write about?

What do you want to have accomplished by the end of your writing career?

What are some "rules" you already know you want to ignore?

Affirmations

Like visualization, affirmations are an important tool that can help move you toward the life you desire.

Rewrite each of these affirmations two times. Say or write them as often as you need to until you believe them to be true.

I'm a writer.		
There's no limit to what I can achieve with my writing.		
I'm a bestselling author.		
I make a lot of money from my writing.		
My writing matters.		
I'm a confident writer.		
My writing inspires people.		
People stand in line for me to sign their books.		

My horror stories keep people up at night.		
People say to their friends about my book, "You have to read this."		
Readers root for my characters.		
There are no limits to the amount of money I can make with my novel.		
People want to read my writing.		
I'm patient with my writing.		
Revising comes easily to me.		
Other writers seek me out for advice.		
I was born to write books.		
My muse and I are besties.		

"Creativity is the greatest rebellion in existence."
-Osho

If you want to be a writer, you'll find the time. If you want to be a writer, you'll find the education and tools to become a better one. If you want to be a writer, you'll build a tribe that's supportive of your dreams and will help you become a stronger artist.

Do you want to be a writer? Are you ready?

"I can't bear art that you can walk around and admire. A book should be either a bandit or a rebel or a man in the crowd."
-D.H. Lawrence

Recommended Reading List

Thrill Me: Essays on Fiction – Benjamin Percy

My Reading Life – Pat Conroy

Scratch: Writers, Money, and the Art of Making a Living – Manjula Martin

Hooked: Write Fiction That Grabs Readers at Page One & Never Lets Them Go – Les Edgerton

Writing Movies for Fun and Profit: How We Made a Billion Dollars at the Box Office and You Can, Too! – Robert Ben Garant & Thomas Lennon

The Happiness Project: Or Why I Spent a Year Trying to Sing in the Morning, Clean My Closets, Fight Right, Read Aristotle, and Generally Have More Fun – Gretchen Rubin

Why We Write About Ourselves: Twenty Memoirists on Why They Expose Themselves (and Others) in the Name of Literature – Meredith Maran

Earth is Hiring – Peta Kelly

You Are a Badass: How to Stop Doubting Your Greatness and Start Living an Awesome Life – Jen Sincero

On Writing: A Memoir of the Craft – Stephen King

Big Magic: Creative Living Beyond Fear – Elizabeth Gilbert

Financial Freedom: A Proven Path to All the Money You Will Ever Need – Grant Sabatier

Manifest Now – Idil Ahmed

Additional Resources

Each day writers are advancing their writing skills and interacting with me and other writers by taking a Rebel Writing Course. To find out more about Rebel Writing Courses, please visit: RebelWritingCourses.com.

If you are interested in working with me or reading more of my writing, please visit my website: LibbyCopa.com

About the Book

You're a rebel—write like one.

Do you live life on your own terms? Then write brave! Express yourself in the way you were born to create.

This workbook is designed to reconnect you with what made you want to be a writer in the first place, help you identify self-sabotaging beliefs, set goals, and manifest the creative life of your dreams.

If you're ready to make changes to your creative practice and push yourself to unlock new ways of building your writer life, Rebel Writer's Workbook is here to guide you to your true creative path.

About the Author

Libby Copa is a writer, adventurer, rebel, and aspiring nomad with a mission to connect with rebel writers around the world. For over a decade she has helped and encouraged other creators as an editor and writing coach. She lives in Minnesota, for now.

Twitter: @EditorLibby
Instagram: RebelWritingCourses
Pinterest: RebelWritingCourses

Made in the USA
Middletown, DE
06 January 2021